INTERGALACTIC QUEST

KIDNAP IN SPACE

PETER MILLIGAN

A Purnell Book

Text and illustration © The Mushroom Writers' and Artists' Workshop, London 1986.
Produced by Mushroom Books Ltd for Macdonald and Co (Publishers) Ltd.

First published in UK 1986 by Macdonald and Co (Publishers) Ltd. A BPCC PLC company.

Typeset by Centra Graphics Ltd, London.
Origination FE Burman, London.
Printed and bound by Mondadori, Italy.

Macdonald and Co (Publishers) Ltd, Greater London House,
Hampstead Road, London NW1 7QX.

British Library Cataloguing
in Publication Data

Milligan, Pete
Kidnap in Space.—
(Intergalactic Quest; 3)
I. Title II. Series
823'.914 (J) PZ7

ISBN 0-361-07243-0

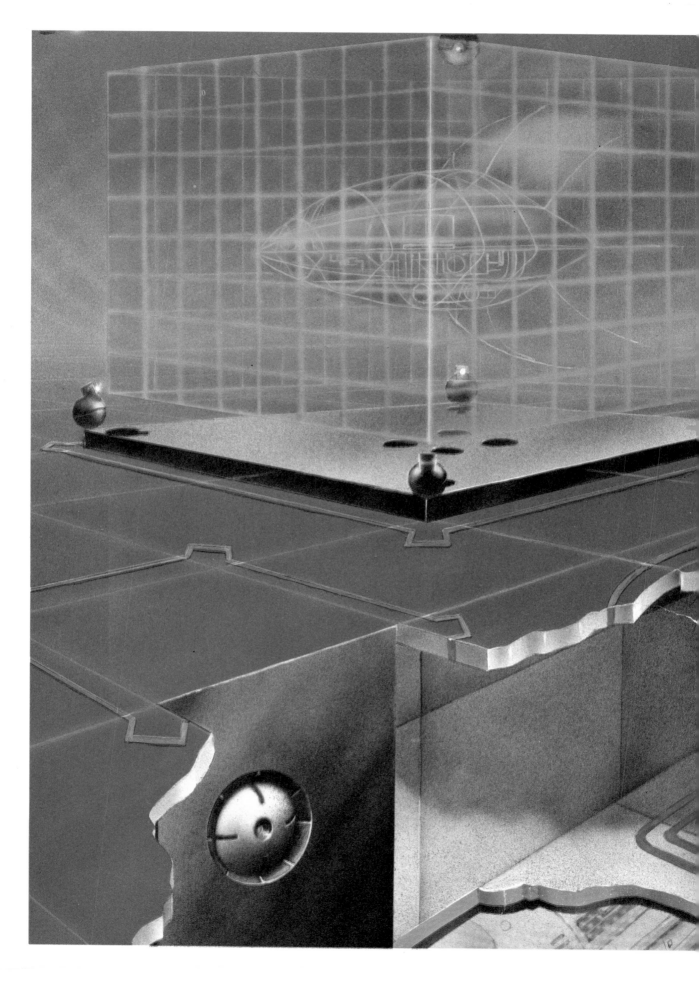

Hello, Earth creature. We are presently travelling at approximately twice the speed of light through the galaxy you call Andromeda. I suppose you want some explanations, right?

My name is RJ66. I am the artificial intelligence that controls the ship in which you are now flying. I was created in the far-off Library of Kos. The planet Kos is one of the most advanced civilizations in the cosmos. It sent me out into the big, bad universe to accomplish a number of missions. But my decision-making instruments have malfunctioned. I might be a hyper-intelligent computer, but I can't deal with the unexpected, the random or the bizarre. That's where you come in.

I scanned your planet and determined that you were the person best suited to join me. So I teleported you up, put you into suspended animation and implanted a module inside your brain. This module allows us to communicate telepathically. It also allows you to understand any of the strange alien languages you're likely to meet out there.

The ship you are flying in is the culmination of centuries of research. It has two remarkable qualities. The first of these is that you are actually linked to the ship, so when the ship is hit, you feel pain, and when my sensors detect danger, you feel fear. The second quality is that the ship is equipped with a replication system. This enables the ship to assume the shape of any object you, as the ship's decision-maker, tell it to.

If you want to join me on my journey through the universe, take a deep breath and get ready to embark upon an intergalactic quest . . .

CURRENT MISSION: the planet Glynnir is plagued by space pirates who inhabit a nearby artificial planet called Hadezz. Only one thing stops Glynnir being overrun: a repulse shield that covers the planet and destroys any enemy craft trying to land.

The planet was relatively secure until one of the royal courtiers to the queen of Glynnir helped the pirates kidnap her son, Prince Meelo. The ransom the pirates demand is the repulse shield!

Your mission is to thwart the **KIDNAP IN SPACE!**

You have been in suspended animation. Now you wake and RJ's voice inside your head explains the situation. "To save the heir, Prince Meelo, we are journeying into the pirates' planet, Hadezz. Once in there, you will be teleported down into their stronghold. Your task is to find the prince and give him a teleportation belt. Then I will be able to teleport you both aboard. Remember, though, to teleport you up, I have to use my replication system to change back into my normal ship form, so this might not always be safe. At the moment, we are flying into the hollow pirate planet, in the shape of a space-junk."

Before you is a confusion of ships and floating buildings.

RJ quickly locates the pirate stronghold. "The prince is in there somewhere," RJ tells you.

RJ explains that there are a number of small tunnel-like entrances to the stronghold. There are also a number of guard ships cruising around. You have two options: you can either be teleported straight into the stronghold, and risk materializing in a dangerous situation, or you can try to crawl through one of the tunnels and hope it leads somewhere.

If you want to teleport in, go to page 24.

Or if you want to take one of the tunnels, crawl to page 13.

You creep round the corner. And immediately receive a thundering blow to the head.

"Filthy sneakgabbler!" cries Metal-mask, towering above you. "No one stalks me!"

Your mind works quickly. If you could get the teleportation belt around Metal-mask's waist, you could take him back to the ship and exchange him for Prince Meelo.

'You've been reading too many fairy tales,' thinks RJ. 'This brute is powerful. You can't handle him like you did the courtier. Your best chance is to try to outrun him. His huge bulk will probably make him slow.'

"So where do I run?" you gasp, avoiding Metal-mask's hands as they try to grab you.

"There's a small alcove to your left. It's so small Metal-mask won't be able to follow you into it."

If you want to try to get the belt around Metal-mask's waist, go to page 3.

Or if you want to slip into the alcove, go to page 15.

You are no match for the fiery Metal-mask. He batters you to near unconsciousness, and then you are carried to a higher level of the pirate stronghold where a crowd of rough and rowdy space pirates have gathered to watch you walk the plank.

As you stand quivering on the plank, you look down at the hollow planet of Hadezz. "What are those strange things flying around?" you ask.

"Ha!" bellows Metal-mask. "Those are fetoid fish-birds. They keep the planet clean by eating rubbish like you. Now jump!"

"What do I do?" you ask RJ.

"You could leap off the plank," comes RJ's reply. "I might be able to get to you before the fetoid fish-birds. It's risky though."

"So what else can I do?"

"You could try teleporting aboard, but I'm being inspected by some rather mean-looking ships at the moment. I have to change from this space-junk shape to normal ship form to teleport you aboard, and these pirates might have enough fire-power to destroy us."

"That's a great help, RJ," you say, as Metal-mask begins prodding you with an electro-spear.

Do you jump? Go to page 9.

Or do you try to teleport up? Go to page 21.

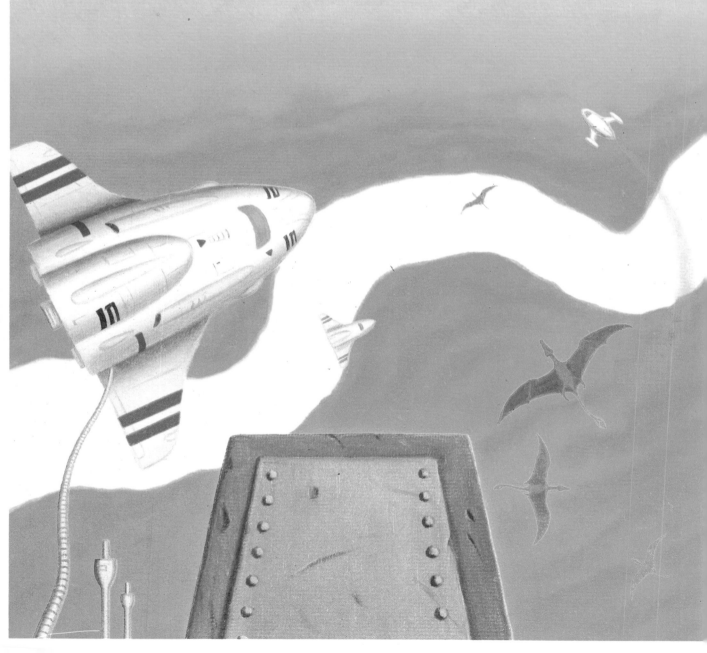

The toe of your boot slips on some slime and you fall over. 'Ouch!' thinks RJ. 'I felt that. You should be more careful, Earth-thing.'

'Shut up!' you think, catching your breath. There, before you, is an unspeakably disgusting creature, skulking and sniffling its way towards you like a great, fleshy, monstrous vacuum-cleaner.

"It's a carbonviper," RJ tells you. "It sucks the carbon from all carbon-based beings, like *you*! It's impossible to kill a carbonviper, but you can put some of its segments out of action. Its radar segment lets it find prey in the dark. Its sucker segment extracts the carbon from its victims."

Which segment should you hit with your laser?

The radar segment? Go to page 28.

Or the sucker segment? Go to page 11.

You find yourself in a huge armoury full of weird and wonderful weapons.

"Some of this stuff might be useful," you say, as you reach for the nearest piece of hardware.

"Don't touch," orders RJ. "They might be booby-trapped."

You're just about to moan about this, when you hear a strange crackling noise coming from a large bomb-shaped structure standing in the centre of the armoury.

"If you'd like to investigate it at closer range I might be able to tell you what it is," says RJ.

As you're trying to decide whether or not to investigate the structure, you hear the sound of footsteps and muffled voices. RJ says, "Sensors indicate two persons walking down an adjoining corridor."

If you want to follow these footsteps, go to page 7.

Or if you want to check out the noise coming from the bomb-shaped structure, go to page 21

After freeing the prince and placing the teleportation belt around his waist, you are both teleported up to the ship. But the ship has to revert to its normal shape to do this and it is seen and attacked by space-junks.

The hollow planet is suddenly ablaze with gunfire. You head for the planet's exit, dodging some shots and flinching as others find their targets. "A slower or weaker ship would be destroyed in seconds," says RJ.

You clench your teeth, and tears fill your eyes as wave after wave of space-junk fighters unload their weapons at you.

"I can't take much more," you groan. "Can't we try changing back to a space-junk? With luck they'll lose sight of us and think we are one of them."

If you want to change from your normal ship form to that of a space-junk, go to page 21

If you want to bite the bullet and keep heading for the exit as you are, go to page 19.

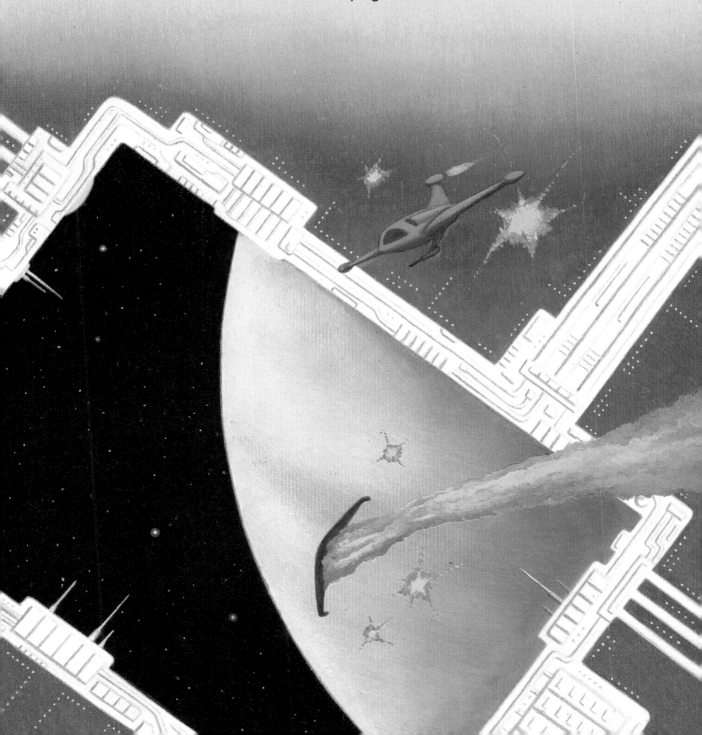

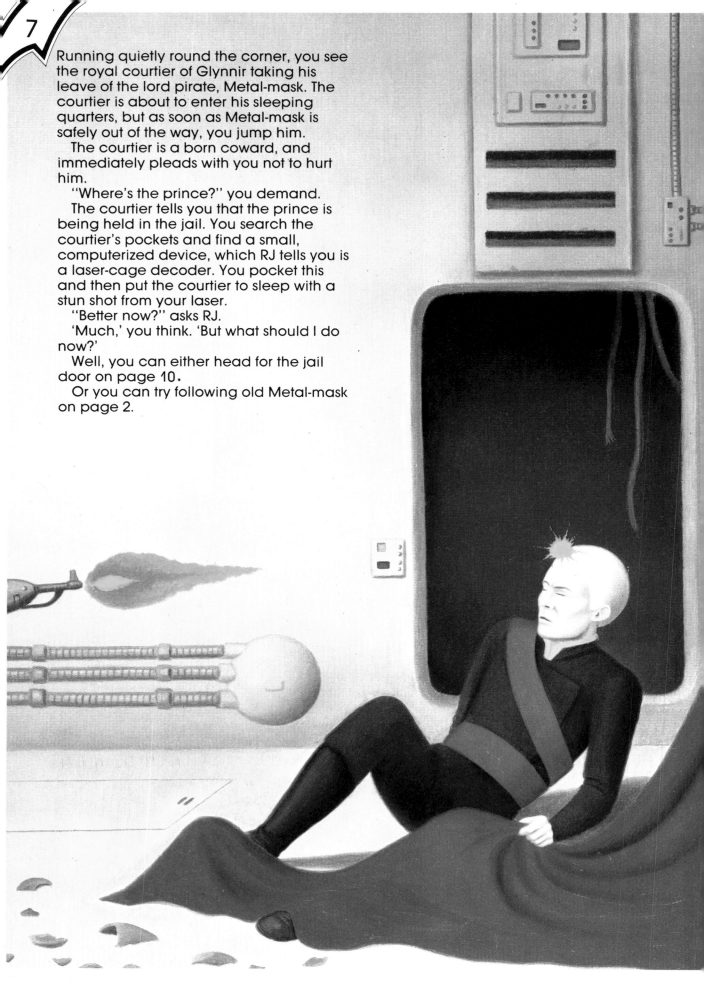

Running quietly round the corner, you see the royal courtier of Glynnir taking his leave of the lord pirate, Metal-mask. The courtier is about to enter his sleeping quarters, but as soon as Metal-mask is safely out of the way, you jump him.

The courtier is a born coward, and immediately pleads with you not to hurt him.

"Where's the prince?" you demand.

The courtier tells you that the prince is being held in the jail. You search the courtier's pockets and find a small, computerized device, which RJ tells you is a laser-cage decoder. You pocket this and then put the courtier to sleep with a stun shot from your laser.

"Better now?" asks RJ.

'Much,' you think. 'But what should I do now?'

Well, you can either head for the jail door on page 10.

Or you can try following old Metal-mask on page 2.

There is a blinding second of pain and light, during which you hear RJ's voice screaming, "Idiot! You've destroyed us!"

You forgot about the planet's repulse shield! It destroys all pirate junks attacking the planet. And you were in the form of a pirate junk!

As you drift into blackness, you hear RJ's dying lament. "Why didn't I get a nice young Ventriugian creature to help me instead of this useless humaaaaaaan . . ."

Your head feels as though twenty robotic midgets are dancing on your scalp. You open your eyes — and see twenty robotic midgets dancing on your scalp.

"Hello," says RJ's familiar voice. "I hope you're enjoying your robotic head-massage."

"It's wicked. What's happening?"

"Your forthcoming mission to save Prince Meelo is a highly important one, so to increase your chances of success I formulated a series of possible scenarios you may or may not have to deal with. I hope you have learned something from this."

"You mean the adventure I've just been through was all inside my head?"

"Implanted images that can be altered by your decision-making. Boy, did you make some silly blunders!"

"Okay, clever clogs. We can't all be mega-intelligent beings from distant galaxies. When do we start the mission for real?"

You start it right now, on page 1.

After thrashing the half-asleep guards, you get to the door of the jail. "Just think," you say to RJ, "behind this door is our goal! Our journey's end!"

"Have you a key?" RJ asks bluntly.

If you have a key, stop standing there like a lemon and open the door. Go to page 18.

If you don't have a key, how do you expect to open a jail door? You wander off looking for another entrance and come across some more guards about to play a game of rune. Go to page 12.

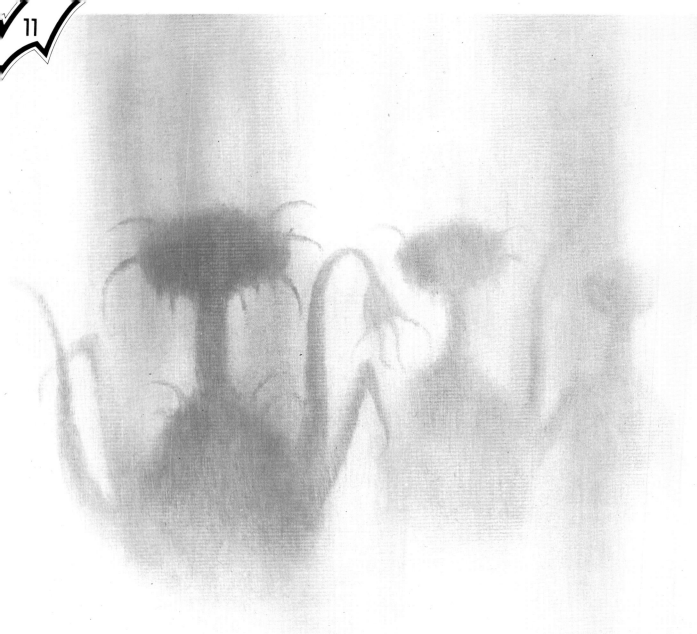

Without its sucker segment, the carbonviper can only slobber over you. 'Disgusting,' you think, as you brush the beast to one side and stride forward.

"Those carbonvipers are a pushover," you declare.

"I wouldn't bet on it," says RJ. You turn and see about twenty of the beasts slithering down the corridor towards you.

"No time to fight," says RJ. "There's an anti-gravity chute up ahead. It's a kind of advanced lift service that takes you to any level of the building. Get in it. *Quick!*"

You step into the anti-gravity chute and immediately feel as though every muscle in your body were being massaged by tiny angel fingers.

"This is no time for bad poetry," RJ snaps. "Tell the chute to take you up or down a level. It will obey your spoken command."

Do you tell the chute to go up? Go to page 29.

Or do you tell it to do down? Go to page 25.

Before the game can begin, the black figure of Metal-mask, Lord of the Pirates, bursts into the room, followed by a few guards.

"You!" he shouts pointing at you. "Foul droggleflaker of an intruder! Get him, me laddies!"

You duck and run as the laser fire crisscrosses the room. Three of the rune players are blocking your exit. You turn round but find Metal-mask in your path.

"You'll have to fight your way out," says RJ.

'But who should I fight?' you think.

If you want to fight the three rune players, go to page 15.

If you want to fight Metal-mask, go to page 3.

You find yourself in a grubby, ill-lit corridor. One sniff tells you that this is space pirate territory. From the distance you hear the sound of rough laughter and wild singing. A shiver runs down your spine.

From one end of the corridor you suddenly hear footsteps approaching. From the other end you hear a shuffling, snuffling sound, and detect a strong animal odour.

"The choice is yours," RJ tells you. "But the lives of many rest on your decision. One foul-up now and it's 'Goodnight, Glynnir!'"

'Very comforting,' you think. 'So which way do I turn?'

If you want to go towards the footsteps, go to page 24.

If you want to go towards the shuffling, snuffling sound, go to page 4.

You shoot old Slugbreath.

"Now you've blown it," says RJ, as the pirate sinks to the floor.

The other pirates stand up. They surround you. They look down at you. Then they smile and applaud. "A fine tactical move," one of them enthuses. "You might be a young 'un but you've all the makings of a first-rate rune player."

They ask if you want to stay for another game.

If you want to stay and play, go to page 12.

Or if you want to continue your search for Prince Meelo, go to page 25.

There is a blinding flash, and you rub your eyes.

"Don't do that. It's bad for them," scolds RJ. "You are merely seeing the effects of a spatio-temporal displacement unit. This works by juxtapositioning . . ."

At this point you stop listening. Five minutes later RJ finishes with the word 'marmalade'. You dread to think what marmalade has to do with anything, so you change the subject by asking what you should do.

"If you'd been listening you would have known. There are two exits. The first exit will lead to the jail where the prince is being held. The second exit will shunt you back in time to somewhere during the last day. You might find youself doing and saying things you've done before, but anything you've picked up on the mission, any key or decoder, will be lost and will have to be found again."

"So," you repeat, "what should I do?"

"Don't ask me. That's anybody's guess."

The first exit? Go to page 18.

Or the second exit? Go to page 13.

You obliterate the faster, less powerful ships, but that still leaves the heavier, armed junks free to unleash shock wave after shock wave of damaging strikes against your ship.

"Another second and we'll be finished," RJ gasps. "We could try changing into one of them. It might confuse them long enough for us to be able to escape."

"Or we could try hyper-spin," you suggest. "We could spin so fast we create our own dimensional vortex, thereby slipping into a new dimensional stream."

"Where did you get all that from?" RJ asks.

"I've been looking at the holo-manual," you reply.

If you want to change into one of the ships, go to page 21.

Or if you want to try hyper-spin, go to page 9.

It's just as well you reverted to normal ship form. In another second, the planet's repulse shield would have destroyed you, as it is now destroying the pirate ships which followed you.

You land by the royal palace and hand Prince Meelo over to his mother, the Queen of Glynnir. The grateful people offer to throw a great banquet in your honour, but RJ declines.

"I want to be clear of this area before the space pirates regroup and make flights through the galaxy even more dangerous," RJ explains. "However, as

soon as I return to the planet of Kos I'll file a report and send a fleet here to rid your galaxy of the pirates once and for all."

As you take off from Glynnir you think about all the food you could be eating. "That's the trouble with being a hero in space," you grumble. "There's never enough time to enjoy the rewards."

"A job well done should be reward enough," says RJ.

'Boy,' you think, 'why do hyper-intelligent beings have to be so dull and boring?'

"What a dump," you say, as you enter the jail. "What did you expect?" says a high-pitched voice. "A ten-star space hotel?"

You spin round and see Prince Meelo. He looks very bored and very spoiled. Surrounding him there is a strange luminous glow emanating from some machinery.

You go to give the prince your teleportation belt.

"That's not much good if you can't get me out of this laser cage, is it?" he squeaks.

"Meelo's right," adds RJ. "We need a laser cage decoder."

If you have a decoder set the prince free and go to page 6.

If you haven't, go and look for one. "The royal courtier has one," Meelo tells you. Go to page 7.

At last, you pass through the exit and break free from the planet. But outside, you see that more pirate space-junks are lying in wait for you. You zap one of them, scoring a direct hit. Then, suddenly, from your left you are attacked by a fleet of heavy, slow, but very powerful junks. From your right you are attacked by a fleet of sleeker, faster, but less powerful ships.

You have time only to destroy one of the fleets.

If you want to destroy the slow, powerful fleet, go to page 23.

Or if you want to destroy the fast, less powerful fleet, go to page 16.

"Yes, Slugbreath. You have the rune," you say.

Slugbreath opens his giant paw. It's empty. "Now I kill you," he grunts.

Luckily, though, all the other pirates also want the pleasure of finishing you off, and while they are fighting among themselves you are able to sneak away. You run along a few corridors and slip out through a porthole.

Your stomach does a quick somersault. You are clinging precariously to the side of the stronghold. Deadly fetoid fish-birds and an assortment of alien craft pass by you .

"Get back inside!" says RJ.

"And face those space pirates! No thanks!"

There's only one thing for it. You'll have to climb to another porthole entrance. There's one about six feet above you, another about six feet below.

Do you want to climb up? Go to page 5.

Or do you want to climb down? Go to page 2.

As the ship changes shape it is blitzed by
the surrounding space-junks. You feel the
pain explode through your every fibre as
the ship is smashed to a pulp.
   And then there is only blackness . . .

Scrambling down the stairs, you catch sight of the old man as he disappears around a corner. You fire your laser at him. As the shot ricochets off the wall, you hear the old man's high-pitched scream.

'Got him,' you think, running round the corner.

"Maybe not," says RJ, as you reach the spot where the old man *should* be . . . but isn't.

He had two possible escape routes. In front of you is an anti-gravity chute, a kind of elevator that uses an anti-gravity device to shunt you to the different layers of the pirate stronghold. To your right is a door hanging half off its hinges. The anti-gravity chute is humming, suggesting it has just been used. You could ask the chute to take you to where its last customer alighted.

"It could be a trick though," says RJ. "He might have gone through that door."

If you want to go through the door, go to page 29.

If you want to take the anti-gravity chute, go to page 27.

You blitz the heavier ships. The faster ships swarm about you, but their poor firepower causes you only slight discomfort. A few mini-nukes send them scuttling.

You outrun the rest of the space-junks, hurtle across space, and soon are approaching the planet Glynnir. Then RJ informs you that a fleet of pirate space-junks is approaching from deep space. They will not know anything about your trip to Hadezz, so you change to space-junk form before they have you in their sights.

Thinking you are one of them, the new space-junks ignore you. But as you continue to approach Glynnir some of them join you, presuming you to be on a pillaging raid.

Do you keep flying in junk form and hope the pirates turn back? Go to page 8.

Or do you revert to normal ship form and risk being attacked again? Go to page 17.

Above you and below you twist the skeletal shapes of spiral staircases. But the gloom obscures your view.

Suddenly, a decrepit old space pirate stomps up the stairs and, seeing you, draws his hand gun.

"What are you doing here then?" he barks.

You think fast. "Oh, yeah, I've just been to look at the prince child."

An evil, toothless grin breaks across the old spacedog's face. "You is nothin' but a child thing yourself. An' pretty soon you'll be a dead 'un!"

With that, he lifts his hand gun. But you have anticipated this and your hand is already on your laser. You remember that your laser is set on kill mode.

If you want to change the setting to stun and knock the old man unconscious, go to page 26.

Or if you think it is too dangerous to let him live, use the gun on kill setting, go to page 27.

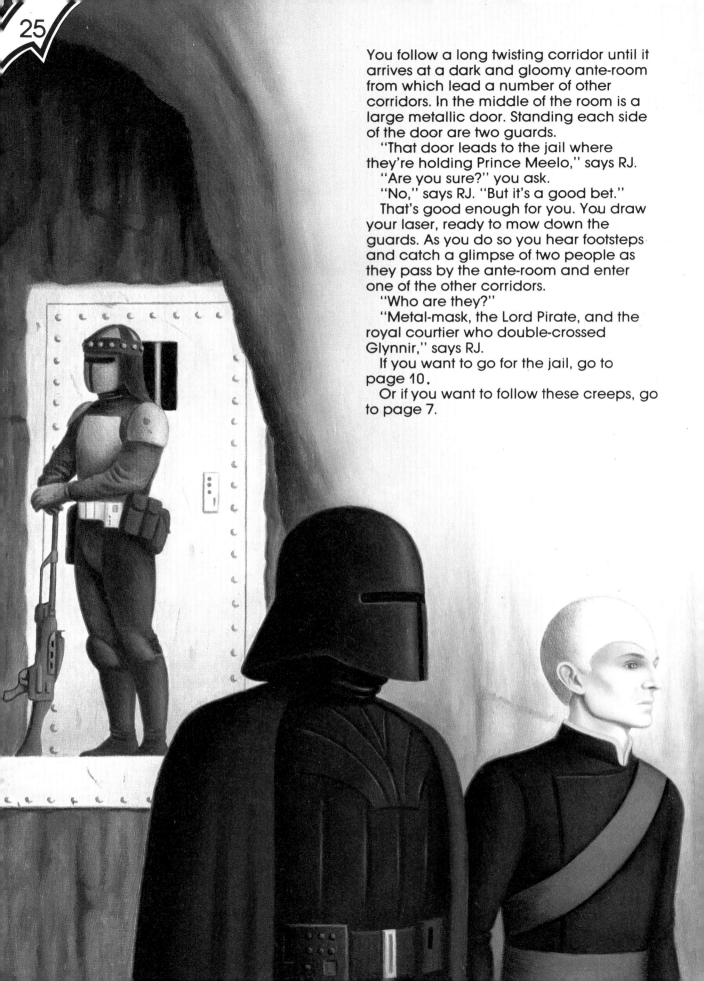

You follow a long twisting corridor until it arrives at a dark and gloomy ante-room from which lead a number of other corridors. In the middle of the room is a large metallic door. Standing each side of the door are two guards.

"That door leads to the jail where they're holding Prince Meelo," says RJ.

"Are you sure?" you ask.

"No," says RJ. "But it's a good bet."

That's good enough for you. You draw your laser, ready to mow down the guards. As you do so you hear footsteps and catch a glimpse of two people as they pass by the ante-room and enter one of the other corridors.

"Who are they?"

"Metal-mask, the Lord Pirate, and the royal courtier who double-crossed Glynnir," says RJ.

If you want to go for the jail, go to page 10.

Or if you want to follow these creeps, go to page 7.

"You wouldn't have lasted five minutes in Earth's old Wild West," mocks RJ, for as you fumble to change your laser setting to stun, the old pirate fires at you.

The spacedog's aim is as terrible as his breath, but you still have to duck. This gives him time to nip off down the staircase, cackling like the madman he is.

"Maybe you should follow him," suggests RJ.

'It's all right for you,' you think back. 'You just sit up there dishing out the good advice. It's me who has to do all the leg work.'

You feel a short sharp jab behind your left ear. Evidently, RJ doesn't like being argued with.

If you want to follow the mad old space pirate, go to page 22.

Or if you want to start climbing the stairs, go to page 29.

For a moment you are blinded by a sudden flash of light. When your vision clears you see the old man crumpled on the floor in front of you, gasping his last breath.

"Sorry, old fella," you say, "but that's life."

"Actually," remarks RJ, "that's death. I would advise you to take the key from around the old man's neck. It would seem he was Prince Meelo's jailer. If that is the case, the key might be useful."

You take the key. 'But will the jail be in the lower regions of the stronghold or the upper?' you wonder.

"You mean," says RJ, "was the old jailer going to or coming from the prince when you bumped into him?"

The old man had been coming up the stairs, but that doesn't necessarily mean anything. Can you remember what was said between you and the old man? And will it help you to make the right decision?

If you want to look in the upper regions of the stronghold, go to page 29.

Or if you want to look in the lower regions, go to page 4.

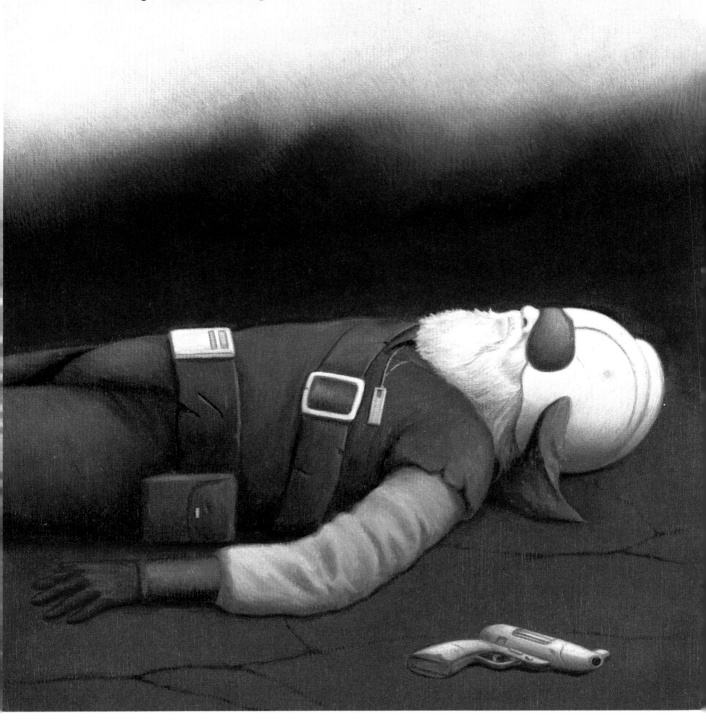

You destroy the carbonviper's radar segment. But it isn't dark, is it? So it doesn't need radar to find you.

"Stupid!" says RJ, as the beast leaps at you, sending you sprawling onto the floor and your laser spinning out of your hand. As the carbonviper dives in for the kill, you roll out of the way.

"There's a doorway up ahead," says RJ, as you leap to your feet, avoiding yet another lunge from the viper. "You might be able to outrun the viper."

Out of the corner of your eye you see your laser lying on the ground. "Maybe I should try to get to the laser and shoot its sucker segment instead," you say.

Do you try to get to the laser and shoot at the carbonviper's sucker? Go to page 11.

Or do you try to outrun it down the corridor? Go to page 5.

After a while you arrive at a room where a gang of tough pirates are playing some kind of game. They mistake you for a young pirate and ask if you want to play a game called rune.

"It's a traditional space pirate game," RJ tells you. "To refuse to play is taken as a declaration of war."

"Let's play!" you announce.

For the next half-hour you play the pirates at rune. You're not sure what's going on, but by a mixture of beginner's luck and a few helping hands from RJ you manage to play quite well.

Eventually a space pirate called Slugbreath speaks to you.

"It's just me and you now," he says threateningly.

"What does he mean?" you ask RJ.

"If I remember correctly, one of you will lose the game. You have to guess whether or not Slugbreath is holding a rune in his hand. If you guess incorrectly, you lose the game.

"And then what?"

"Oh, didn't I tell you? The loser is killed. My advice is to guess that he has the rune. Fun, isn't it?"

Do you follow RJ's advice and say, "Yes, Slugbreath. You have the rune"? Go to page 20.

Or do you shoot old Slugbreath between the eyes, regardless of the fact that there are several of his chums surrounding you? Go to page 14.